Late Rapturous

Also by Frank X. Gaspar

Late Rapturous

poems

Frank X. Gaspar

AUTUMN
HOUSE PRESS

PITTSBURGH

Autumn House Press receives state arts funding support
through a grant from the Pennsylvania Council on the
Arts, a state agency funded by the Commonwealth of
Pennsylvania, and the National Endowment for the Arts,
a federal agency.

ISBN: 978-1-932870-60-2

Library of Congress Control Number: 2011945148

Contents

three

—And as we went down the hill the devil began to describe to me with animation the cults and feasts and religions that flourished in his youth. All that coast of the Great Green then, from Byblos to Carthage, from Eleusis to Memphis, was crowded with gods. Some of them astonished men by their perfect beauty, others by their complicated ferocity; but all took part in the life of men, making it divine; they journeyed in triumphal cars, breathed the scent of flowers, drank wind, loved sleeping maidens. That is why peoples emigrating might leave their flocks and forget the rivers at which they had drunk, but would lovingly carry their gods with them in their arms.

—Eça de Queirós

Close your mouth
Block off your senses
Blunt your sharpness
Untie your knots
Soften your glare
Settle your dust

—*Tao te Ching*

One

June/July—Eleven Black Notebooks at the Desert Queen Motel

Then night again. The dry lightning like artillery over the far reefs
of stone and the thunder-god shearing the air—*all* the gods in foment
and calamity, but it is not enough. The rumble and rupture, the shattering.
Out there in the wilderness. Isaiah, Ezra, their lamentations, insufficient
in the madness, and me with my tall can of iced beer leaning
at the railing outside my door, like at the taffrail of a ship, but instead
of the big turbines thrumming on blackoil, now only the small throats
of the air conditioners gagging and moaning. The cold aluminum sweats
in my hand, and I'm pleased for this small miracle, water out of the
cracked desert air, but it is not enough. My happiness now, with the
work coming forth in fits and then gouts, is not enough, for it saves
nothing, yet it is a happiness after all, and therefore inexplicable.
The stars crowd one another out of their familiar lines. The arm
of the galaxy, its bright muscle against the belly of the sky. Not enough.
My heart full or empty, not enough. Now, to set something down in
the midst of folly, one true word, one simple cry out of the black arroyos
and dangerous washes, the canyons, the granite redoubts, but the lone sob
of the desert hen is not enough, the television's mangled voices creeping
through the drywall and stucco are not enough, and I am running out of
time and money, always time and money. And love, I don't forget love,
but it's not enough either, it doesn't save anything, the graves open for all
the beloved to lie down in and all the despised as well, and it is still not enough.
Stepping back into the cramped room I think of that ship again. How a ship will
fit into the poem at this juncture. Perhaps my own ship from that other time.
One hundred thousand tons of death and empire. Grand under my feet. Rolling
with the long ocean swells. Sky like desert sky, shot with the unutterable trillions.
And the engines banging forward blindly. Into that darkness. Under that blaze.

Sometimes God Saves the Fire

And I would light myself afire for a poem if I thought it would
light *you* afire, the way I dreamed once that the river burned
beyond 10th Avenue, and the young girls came selling their roses
and carnations all along the banks, while the black smoke rolled
into the sky, and the people crowded the buildings' roofs and iron
ladders and watched with their hands shading their naked eyes.
What was it that made this life seem like just one long convalescence
from a nameless plague brought over from an island on the other
side of sleep? I don't remember passage on any ship. I stole among
the living, weak and unknown, the drift and rhapsody of the avenues,
the shadow-buildings lining the canyons of the lateral streets, glass
and brick everywhere, streets where a king might walk, offering you
small gifts, though none ever came. When you find your heart is no
longer high and pure, can you say it ever was? My abiding shame.
Sitting in solitude that winter without human comfort among pads
of cheap onion paper and second-hand books. What kind of freak?
That city once. That West Side with all its little markets and ghosts
and doom. Those long poems, if that's what they ever were, all lost,
and the old black Underwood, too, its frayed ribbon and glass keys
and every thread and artifact. And now, fires unto fire, here
in L.A., the long whistle of a train heading down to the port, 4:13 AM,
lying awake, rolling fog, and I'm still wandering in the chronic rage
under the vanished awnings of 10th Avenue, all its closed doors and
lost nights. What am I therefore who would raze whole cities for you
if I only had the power in my stuttering hands? 10th Avenue, five floors,
how I would walk up the sagging stairs, the banisters hand-worn to
a dull shine, the little room, the window sill's infatuate grit, the ancient
radiator, its creamy paint, its glaze and ticking, all the fire and all the
resurrections—a poster taped to the closet door, the cluttered table by
the narrow bed, a hallway of dreams and fever, a small lamp burning.

Then Saint Francis Blessed the Creatures

Maybe it was Amsterdam or Brussels, this dream, for
there was all this art and light everywhere, and grassy
parks with unnamable flowers and the young embracing
in the shadows, but speaking, too, in a language that was
familiar and yet opaque to me, and I stood leaning on
the gates of hell with a cigarette in my mouth, and some
trees were on fire and they resembled lilies in their white
eternal flames, and I knew it appeared to the others that
I was callously watching the world unravel, and no one
invited me or nodded in my direction or said anything
civil, as though it were my fault that so much wonder
and happiness lay in all directions and they just didn't
know about it. Well, you wake up from *that* at four a.m.
and you have a choice—this world or the other one. It's
still dark outside, and your head is pounding, and your
tongue is parched, and bells are tolling everywhere and
horses are stamping and snorting under the windows,
down in the street. It's all very dangerous. If you lay your
burdens down you just might miss them, and then you'll be
stuck with some stupid yearning for the rest of your life.
For myself, I took down my walking cane and went to
the kitchen and turned on the lamp in the cupboard and
gazed at the boxes and cans, their brilliance and symmetry
rising from the confusion. Pretty soon I started making up
aphorisms and maxims that I hoped to live by. Pretty soon
the street would be full of birds and all their predawn racket.
They are so pure in their imperatives. I ran some water
over my hands. You really do think for a moment that
the birds are singing, maybe singing to one another
or even to you. That's putting a good face on it. And why
not? Have some coffee. It's not too early for that. And

then when the first graying comes and the porch and grass
are wet and cold, go on out with a heaving mug of it, sweet
and thick with milk and get that cold damp earth under your
naked feet. And listen. Listen hard enough to that singing
and then you won't ever call it that again, whatever it is
that comes from all those greedy throats. And then in
the headlands and pastures of your city you can join the beasts.
They are all like you. They are all crying. They are all hungry.
They are all dying for something. For just about anything.

Sycamore

Sometimes none of us is thinking straight. It's all right, I know,
but you forget sometimes that you're not in charge of the world,
and you want to make a difference. Prayer flags, for instance,
slowly starving themselves into string with their incessant
whispering into the void from whence they were born. In my
dear friends' yard, I mean, and we are walking in the full Eden
of it, acres of it, lavender and peppermint and a kind of basil,
and morning glories, and hickory trees, all tall and iron-looking,
and several kinds of oaks, and tall clutching pines. You would go
dizzy with the naming. And the forest creek and cambered clay road
and wood-peckers in their serious percussions, and the serpents
abounding—eighteen copperheads in one year—and the air is plain
and wet and dense, and we come upon an arbor and another crescent
of prayer flags. A poem about truth. A poem about the transitory
nature, not of just you but of everything. Not a concept, not an idea,
just more little flags now limp in the breeze, fading in the radiance.
If the roof of the world is a wheel, if the heart of the world is a heart,
then you have another poem about truth, and if that's the case
you had better not trust it, not trust its voice or its knowing vowels,
or its perfumed arrogance. We've all been down that road, and it
leads to the edge of a town with one broken-down gasoline station
and its pile of yellowed ledgers, and one sad ghost wondering where
the glory days have slipped off to. That is not the way. We walked along
a gully and over a downed sycamore and then back to the house, and
we found someone cooking gumbo among stacks of books. There are
some moments you cannot live in. A poem about beauty. It always
places you directly outside something, and even so, you are charmed
and do not think of this as cruelty. No, we entered the house. We loved
everyone. Our hearts were bursting. The heart of the earth. It is a heart.
Warm bread. Hot steaming bowls. We talked and talked. All those words
around our glowing heads. Isn't that what we make that world with?

Wail for Her

Put off your prison garments and dine at the king's table
until the day of your death as long as you live. Never mind
the grammar. It's written. It's written also: Your hurt is un-
curable, and your wound is grievous. This in the second day
of the summer's heat wave, the city frogs peeping in their
lawless fens, traffic buzzing at midnight, something grinding
out there in the flushed darkness beyond the open pane of my skylight.
Jeremiah again. Perfect for the fevers. I am dining on a cold beer
and potato chips. I am at the part again where Babylon had once
been a golden cup in the Lord's hand, making all the earth drunken
but suddenly She is broken. It is all too much to take in. The new cat
chases the old cat in dizzy raptures, they come to me and chew the edges
of my wilted books and papers. Nothing adds up. Are you still
looking for the one soul to complete you? Are you still searching
with that kind of faith you once had when you were young and
immortal, with your quick eye and that smooth muscle, with the easy
balm of all that promise and hope? Sometimes you see him out of the
corner of your eye just getting into his black car in the parking lot
by the drugstore—oh, the heat, he is wearing a shirt cut off at the
shoulders, and dark glasses—that much stays with you. Or sometimes
she turns her head in just a certain way, fleeting, always fleeting,
in the aisle in the supermarket, or running on one of those flat
paths in the park—the sun is so heavy, her bare arms are damp and
glistening. It's no use, the heart began its howling in the womb,
I don't believe it will ever stop. The fans whir sweetly. The air
kisses the thin pages with languor and dissipation. I didn't break
the golden cup. I didn't ask for all this wandering. How long? How long?
Soon, soon, says the heart, even as its own time strikes away. Out
in the shadowy yard you can hear a million wings thrashing, the air is hot
and wild, the moon has been waning for weeks, and just now you think
you glimpse its barest sliver of light, but in the time it takes to turn
and look, there's only the sky, whole and black and walled with stars.

I Wander Down My Street Because I Cannot Find a Book

The television gives rain, but it's California, so one can never be sure.
How many times do we have to go through this, the perky-*cum*-serious
girls with the beefy microphones at their lips, the ludicrous foul-weather
gear? They tell us it could rain, it could be a disaster, the storm, the storm,
though they are dry, not even a breeze in the quiet palms behind them,
and I am trying to find out exactly where Rilke wrote that sentence about the
young girls, drawing or maybe painting, suppressing the inalterable hidden life
that their art brings forth, though I doubt I have his language right, and all
my Rilke has suspiciously gone missing, I've turned everything upside down,
it's useless and terrifying this crazy forgetting that creeps up on me. Outside
the skies have turned the color of an old spoon, and I can walk under the arch
of tree limbs between here and the park, that inner life, with its black river and
its ragged boatman, and the music of the spheres, its shames, its glories—you
don't forget it, it's true, it can't be altered—and the park is rowdy —softball,
old guys yelling, binking the slow-pitch with their aluminum bats, and Lupe
selling her tamales from the big blue Igloo cooler. I take a half-dozen, two
chile-cheese, two sweet, two chicken—the mothers are out with their dogs, I
wave, they wave, I make a slow circuit along the narrow paving, pines and
magnolias, purple cherry, a handbill for a lost cat, basketballs pounding the
hardwood in the rec building, shouts, boys and girls in hoodies and beanies
leaning on a Toyota, tall beers in paper bags, Orpheus thumping in the bass
speakers, Eurydice and all the little queens of the dead—what are they holding
down, finally? What are they holding back, shining as they do under the iron
clouds, shining under those banks of lights over the softball diamond, rhine-
stones on the grass, sequins on the sidewalk, it's coming down this time, it's
starting, blotches spatter the windshields, there's that moment when the smell
of wet dust and oil rises from the pavement, oh terrible angels, oh failing mind
with all the dark spots that once remembered so much, everyone is running!

These Are the Last Good Days of the Republic

That blue chill comes down the street and I can see
the mountains, I can see the snow caped over their shoulders
bright as a drum all those miles away, and winter in the sycamores here,
limbs gray and stripped—they dream of the crows, I can tell,
but no one here knows where they have flown. What
I mean is that the light in the sky is low and full of terror now,
the small wild things dance in it, the police cars, when they come
to the neighbors' house across the way, announce their importance
by arriving in clusters and parking backwards. He is a small man, my
neighbor, old, with one arm and three languages. He made his fortune
in furniture until something happened and now, despite the surgeries,
he wanders and raves, he sneaks cigarettes on the front steps when
he thinks his wife isn't looking. Today he is violent again and wants
to drive his car. It's forbidden, but no one can stop him. He wants to
go and look for his grandson who has gone off to the wars. He will not
listen that the wars are in a different place, far away. The police
stand around in the driveway, they talk with him, sometimes for an hour.
I don't understand their function, but I don't ask too much when I speak
with his wife later. She is weary and she hangs her weight on me, which
is fine with me, she lists her medications, we stand in her wild yard. Her
accent is pleasant, like a shiny nail striking a piece of tin, lightly. *Good days
and bad days,* she says. Her eyes are gray and blue, her pale hair clings
in tight curls. Her husband smokes a cigarette, quiet now, right in front of her.
The light is bluing all around them, the blue chill, the bare sycamores.
Sometimes late at night I see her kitchen lamp burning. Sometimes she
forgets I have my own trees and brings me dark winter oranges. She leaves
them on the doorstep in plastic bags, tied at the top with impossible knots,
I have to cut them open with a knife.

All Dharmas Are Marked with Emptiness

I'm talking now about the destitute and the wild-eyed, I'm
talking about the lady who made the head of the Virgin Mary
out of cut up pieces of magazines and broken glass and a
can of carpenter's glue—and then there's the girl I know
who works in the supermarket, who printed an entire anthology
of poems on a single eight-and-a-half-by-eleven sheet of
Xerox paper and folded a hundred copies down to wallet size
and passed them out to anyone who dared look her in the eye.
You know what I mean: there are all those lonely, desperate,
weird minds—yours among them for all I know—and the
Dharma is everywhere, books and words and people thinking,
beat-up notebooks from the dollar store, scribbling the world
into them—a man has a mystery, a woman has an adventure,
the kids are banging rhymes together like tin cans full of
old nails. Where's it all going, this clatter, this wonder,
this rant against anguish? I tell myself to stay calm. I tell
myself to step back and take a breath. I twist and shift in my
tall black chair. I can hear the city coming in through the kitchen's
window-screens. Night birds, crickets in the unseasonable heat,
some might say dead souls keening in their rivers of fire or
choirs of angels out in the eucalyptus trees, but beyond it all you
hear nothing but the deep nothing—or maybe that's the far-off roar
of a motorcycle: If the night is just right, if the moment is perfect,
you know as well as I do that you don't need to tell the difference.

The Sermon of Saint Anthony to the Fish
(preached in São Luís do Maranhão, 1654)

Wind off the harbor at five A.M. Sky still black in the west-facing
window, already the little streets are sounding with work—metal
banging on concrete down at the docks, an engine, a distant whistle
high and thin. Here in my attic rooms I am pacing and sitting with
Saint Anthony as he talks to the fish. He has turned away from his
congregation since they do not ever listen to him. He turns his
back on them. He summons the fish. They come. They are such
charmed fish. They listen and nod with their heads just out of
the water. They wiggle their tales. They are rapt. *The first thing
that distresses me about you fish,* he says, *is that you eat each other!*
I open the windows over my bed and then the windows over the
table and the breeze is snappy and rinses right on through, over
the planks and under the angled eaves. That's how funny Saint
Anthony is. He does not like the octopus, but one has to mark that
off to a certain temporal prejudice—all that sneaky changing of
color and all those weird arms—certainly in service of darkness. Oh,
he must use men as parables to the fishes! How else to get them to
see their errors? But in the end he tells all those shining cod, bass,
and haddock that his words will really do them no good, no matter
that they are so attentive and sweet, so responsive and appreciative.
They have no souls, after all. The whole notion of redemption does
not apply, so their sermon can not end in grace and glory for them.
I'm still at it, after coffee, with the sun up, and the wind easily now
in the higher registers of small-craft-warning, though I cannot make
out the pennants from here. Soon the school kids come lining up
across the narrow street. Women yell at them continually, *get on
a line, get on a line.* Then they sing songs. When the children do not
understand something the women yell louder. Then they say things
again in Portuguese. It makes a music under the wuthering maples and
chestnuts and oaks. Now the light is everywhere, and the roof over my
head thumps with wind. The street is adazzle. The day opens up. I make

more coffee. You can always save something. Sometimes the riches pelt over you like a hard rain—you duck your head and try to shelter yourself from them because you don't see them for what they are. Even Saint Anthony, though the fish are not capable of glory, gives them this: *Benedicite, cete et omnis quae moventur in aquis. Praise God because He has created so many of you, Who has distinguished you with so many species, Who has dressed you in such variety and beauty, Who has given you such a vast and pure element, Who, coming into this world has lived among you.* In the end, this seems just about enough for anybody.

Bicycle

A breeze was at my back, the low sun too, and the long shadows
of afternoon ran before me—me and my bicycle, balloon tires humming
over the college walks and then upon the black asphalt of the streets
and boulevards, with the crows looking down from the high weather
of the sweet gums and magnolias and jacarandas. I wore a black helmet
and sunglasses, the day running off behind me, behind me too, the Spanish
buildings, their clay tiles, the big dome of the observatory and its old
Schmidt-Cassegrain that you can see the moons of Jupiter through,
hazy and pulsing above the smog and light-scatter whenever you're
willing to climb up there in the dark. You can be both right and wrong
most of the time, joy gliding over sorrow like those morning fogs that
prowl their way around the neighborhood, hip high, sweetening the fruit,
bathing the wilderness of the lawns and marigolds. It's almost like you *are*
and then you *aren't* in the same instant, something in you crying love, love,
but then you look around, and where are you? You can cry until you're blind
from it, it doesn't matter, and that's when the crows warm up to you. You
understand them, they understand you, and they're calling *hey, hey,* because
they'd like the day to hold something for them, some bone and gristle maybe,
some blood and fur smudged across their long platter that is Clark Avenue,
and if you're me, you're just spinning along on that old dinged-up bike,
yelling, *hey, hey,* right back at them, but only inside your head so you don't
disturb any of the good citizens with your little kisses of madness. And
then what's left except to look around for whatever justice and virtue crouch
behind the iron gates and the rolling hedges—and the shine of the neighborhood's
Chevrolets and Hondas, all the dahlias and azaleas and yellow lilies—they
don't last long, it's all part of the deal—and neither do the upturned skateboards
or the basketball hoop over the blue garage, and I leaned around the corner, all
my servile work behind me, up to the house under the trees, rooms full of books
and poems, and two cats in the bay window—they were eyeing those high limbs
too, and the crows were totally with me now, they saw things from aloft, and

they were calling out, and I bumped up onto the driveway breathing, and I was calling back, but only as a kind of thinking, really, nothing but a silence under that glossy helmet, just in the moment when the sun was shrugging down behind the banks of violet clouds, firing the trunks of the sycamores, tilting the world.

The Early Revelations

To begin, there's the breath, in and out, one world entering
another world and then leaving it again, the golden cord or
the silver cord—I can't remember which, but it goes something
like that—something to keep you moving forward even as
you eat old bread and can't find the right book to fit your hands
on a given night. It's insane, this nervous pecking at the keys,
trying to make something, and underneath it all, the words are
finally only like wands or arrows, and the poems want to tear
into someone's heart regardless of the mess that's there, or clap
someone's soul into the marrow-bone of a tree so you can finally
say "soul" without making everybody nervous. This rain lately.
This gloom and the glorious flogging of the shingles, the battering
at the gutters. I had to drive to the fire station for sandbags and still
the water came, black and slow and smelling of gypsum. Not so bad
all told, but dark angels again, sitting on my chest, so exhilarating,
even as they pressed me down. They don't ever leave. They make
themselves at home. You have to say one thing and mean another,
always, or they don't respect you, and they are dangerous. This is me
in January, brooming the waters out of the garage, opening the doors
and windows to get a draft through, letting things dry out. In the yard,
downed branches, buckets of soggy leaves. In the ocean, the warm
current again, 62 degrees, surf, fourteen feet at some of the northern
breaks, and the young and the strong in their muddy trucks, their
boards and wetsuits, heading for those deeper raptures. Well,
everybody's going off *somewhere*, and none of the roads are long.
Me, I'm headed indoors to read about the ruler of the earth and sky,
The Early Revelations. Lovers Pray Continually, for instance. You can
read that all day while the lightning strikes and the thunder and then
another deluge like nails banging the walls. Familiar words in
surprising order, simple and unknowable. Or the vowelic dazzle

of the Suras, which are always just out of reach to me. The images of water, the filigree of the oasis, the well, paradise in a dry land, Allah the Merciful who cannot be fathomed, who is unbegotten and who does not beget. Mysteries for the forlorn and the housebound. Gasfire in the bricks. The downpour, heedless and unrelenting. The wall of winter darkness. You can almost hear the heavens opening.

Black Notebook #9—Los Angeles—In Bed with an Old Book of Chinese Poetry

Of *course* he was sad. It was night again, but all day long he had been churning at his books, stuck in the same old tired dialectics and categories. Those fraudulent poems came from fraudulent thinking. They became a danger in the world. They made him bleed and toss on his own sheets. Sometimes he felt so broken that he started to believe that he couldn't break any further, and then someone would come and ask him for clarification, or another would say, *I'm confused—you seem contradictory.* He confessed that he had always been a frayed glove filled with shattered glass trying to pass himself off as a hand, and then he'd smile in a certain way, and then *they'd* smile in a certain way. It was unbearable. He always felt that something terrible was going to happen. He began to think that nothing was true. Then he made up his mind to stop all this. He decided to go down to that river where the fisherman's wife says she's looking for a good dream. She says they're hard to find. Then she weeps while the rain falls and drips all night from the eaves. He didn't find god there. He didn't find the self and its deadly sins. It was all about how he'd really be if he turned off the lights and turned down the noise and stopped all that goddamned smiling. The emperor gives a silk glove full of pearls to a lovely woman. She is married. She gives two of them back with a letter. *These two are my tears,* she says. How did she grieve so perfectly? *That's* what he wanted to know. Nothing else mattered. By that river: There's a shack there. The wood is old and bleached. The water swirls by it. Sometimes the wind blows the reeds in tiny circles.

We Darken Things

The moths drifted like snowflakes down among the broken
souls of the white rose tree and the spider's web billowing
in its four nameless colors. The sunlight was trying to shoulder
me aside. I didn't move. I was trying to hold the world together
with my skinny body. I had been there since the beginning,
which was a few hours before, after coffee and sugar at the
right hand of God. For the record: the wheels of eight dreams
were spinning in brass and gold and filled my head with visions,
that same white rose tree, those moths falling like gauze
from their roofed chambers in the little wind. I've spent
too much time in such moments, yet I can't help myself. If
two roads diverge, I take the wrong one and curse the world
for my confusion. I seem to have been born for such adventure.
Advance in small sentences, I tell myself. It's been war my whole
life, and behind the roses and the quiet spiders lie the misery
of children and black fires in the jeweled cities. This is the
way the earth moans for love, which is not so different from
your own heart's low tone, or mine. Maybe it was you who
stood next to me on the sunstruck porch overlooking the
harmless lawn and my little stone Buddha, though you don't
know about me except that you might someday find this tattered
in a canning jar or folded in a slight darkwood box on a cellar shelf.
It was sunny in that particular moment. Yes, maybe it was you,
that shadow, long and narrow in the long narrow light, in the corner
of my eye, at my left shoulder, the same greed and the same
aches. By what means do we darken things, you and I, when
all we've done our whole lives is stumble toward the light?
Even now. Our shadow hearts beating through us, the yellow
flurry of the moths, the thorned flurry of the rose tree, all those
blades and angles of the dying morning, that vagrant dust, that tacit
breathing of the leaves, which jostle so lightly when the wind comes.

Petroglyphs, Black Notebook #6

Your gods are not in this place said the spirit from the wall.
His name was Carbon Dioxide. The man knew that. The spirit
had been caught as a drawing etched in the wall of the little cave
into which the man had crawled, and other spirits and totems
were also on the wall. They all had something to say. The one
who was called Crone said, *I doubt you will leave here. Your own*
breath will confuse you. It was a small cave, and the man was on
his belly and pressed upon by the walls. One spirit was called
Quartz Monzonite. He or she seemed to be the wall itself. *It's*
either a womb or a grave, the spirit said. Then another spoke.
The one with his arms coming out of his body from skewed places,
whose head resembled a sun with wavy lines. His name was Rolex.
You are welcome to stay forever, if you like, or you can leave. But
you don't have much time, he said. The man understood that he
had made a mistake, wiggling all the way back here like this. Warnings
had been posted. But he'd told himself it wasn't a mine shaft or anything.
He had a feeling. And the first spirit was correct. They lived here, too,
in the absence of the *Elohim.* No seraphs. No flaming cherubs.
We hardly see anyone anymore, said the spirits, and the man felt
sorry for them, for they seemed to be drawn so badly, like stick-figures,
all random and cockeyed. *How is your breathing now, honey?* said
the spirit who was called Crone. His lungs felt heavy. The bad air. He kept
forgetting which way was out. It was all black except for the little pencil
of his flashlight. Cooler in here. No snakes. Just the writing on the wall.
But he couldn't turn around. He couldn't raise his head. Who would
choose such a place to inscribe their minds? The belly of a desert tortoise.
The skull of a wild dog. Where was the little hole he had wriggled
through? What had possessed him? I still have work to do, he said,
truly confused and afraid now, for he knew his brain was poisoned.
He believed his life depended on something. He remembered the room,

the papers, the books, but it seemed so far off, so impossible now.
He was foggy with sweat, and the rock was against his skin like razor wire.
Maybe he could bargain. Maybe it was a test, like in a story. I'm going
to tell the world about your power and beauty, he said, though he did not
believe either was true about them. *You might, honey,* said Crone.
He was sure it was Crone, the crude vagina, the long breasts. *You might or
you might not.* She laughed. They all laughed. *If you ever find your way out.*

I Would Be True in My Own Body

This was when I lay under the revenant dazzle of the Perseids, with
the blind stones of the desert at my head and the black sky sweeping
east to west. Celestial fire in its hiss of the summer dying. Alien nickel
and iron from the outer belts of nothingness, vagrant and peregrine,
streaking down to me from the frozen reaches. If a tree had fallen
in the forest. There was so much sadness everywhere in that year
of the earth, and the earth under my bones, the sand and the tumble-
weed, the wind like a door opening and closing. I would be true in my
own body. There would be a truth in the tiny engines of the miraculous.
Something beyond ideas and the shameful and beautiful arguments.
Before sundown the two women crossing the drywash with a big rifle,
heading toward the deep caves and the natural tank in the gullied stone,
shadowed and hidden. Water dripping along the sandstone in four seasons.
Perhaps they tarried and bathed their feet as I had done hours before.
Let's face it, you can't rise and shout in such an hour. The arrows hailing
down from the radiant. The journey from existence to immolation. What
is new that courses the blood now? You think something is chipping away
at the moon, but it is only light and revelation. The seep willow, the Indian
paintbrush, the cottonwood, the broom, all humbled and puzzled under
the flailing sky, and me, too, in my perpetual lament. The scorpion's
footfall scuttle, the brown recluse, its rhinestone eyes, the little noise in
the creosote, moon-eyed rat come to steal anything that shines. Now
and then the empty tent huffs and crackles. Sometimes the dead coals
of the fire almost rise to life again in an orange breath. What if all time
could be measured in nothing but death and love? Then who would
calculate the hours for that pre-dawn moment to come when the world
is neither day nor night? No griefs yet for those shapes that things must
take when darkness goes. And there's no word for that color in the sky.
Not a graying as all the books try to tell you, though the patinas on some
coins approach it. An alloy in some cauldron. The spell still casting now,

falling, only the brightest among them in the coming light. What Aristotle thought was weather. Rain. Snow. Hail. Sleet. Meteor. No gods interfering. Then coffee boiling on the flat stones of the pit, and the galleries of sandstone alight and pinking before the advent blaze of morning. Quiet sky now. What has changed, what ever changes? What *is* the truth? That I walked forth alone into the desert to clean the scales from my eyes, and all through the darkness, the stars in the firmament shivered and fell around me?

Two

Late Rapturous

Well, the cold iron wind and the Hudson River from whence it blew,
thirteen degrees on all the instruments and water in my eyes, but
there was a fire someplace, it made my ears burn and sting, and me
buffoonish in my old dirty down parka that I used to sleep in up
in the Sierras with my little tent in the snow—I'd go in on skis by
myself and write haiku in the candlelight because I believed such
things would improve my inner being. But now I was leaning sideways
walking up to 54th street to finally have a look at the de Koonings. I
don't know what I expected, I don't know what I was looking for exactly,
except that I'd seen too many prints, too many cramped photos, and
I wanted the full brunt of it, that *late rapturous style,* that *sexual
confrontation* that I'd read so much about, the crazy man in the Fourth
Avenue loft before lofts were ever cool, drinking and working, working,
re-working, wrapping paintings in wet newspaper so he could rub things
out the next day and start over and over and over, yes, it was that, I will
admit it, I wanted to stand in the presence of the real thing and feel it—
it's never the aboutness of anything but the wailing underneath it, and
there was a pain behind my heart and some kind of weird music inside
my ears, so that riding up in the escalators, there came a slow panic at
the swirl of a woman's long skirt, or a man's head turned at just the right
moment—no explaining the sources of this, not the smells of body
heat and heavy coats, though I know that every time you run toward
something you love, you run away from it too, you get blinded by the
colors or you miss something important and the moment collapses and
takes whole worlds with it, forever, into some kind of blackness. It was
crowded, that room, but almost everybody was just passing through and
I found I could walk right up to those canvasses, and I believe I could
have laid hands on them before anyone jumped me, but of course I
just leaned and stared. I don't know how long. It didn't matter. What
I needed was to take them with me and slant them against a wall some-
place safe and curl up next to them at night instead of trying to sleep.

It would be the only way. Back outside, I staggered up against the wind
and it blew my tears back, and I finally ducked into a little place selling
hot soup in paper bowls, and everyone was taking something off or putting
something on—they were all talking and moving like they knew absolutely
how to spend every hour of their lives, and not in darkness, either, or in
despair or regret, and when I could see that the winter dusk was running to
silver against the high roofs and towers, I stepped out again into the street,
the shiny cabs cruising and the men and women bundled in long coats and
bright scarves, and the hundreds of windows of the city's dark pavilions each
showing its square of yellow light, and I walked back into that other kingdom.

The Prayer of the Quiet Gaze

It was one of those nights. Maybe I was stranded
or maybe I was just waiting for someone. The town
square was deserted except for scattered couples
holding hands, all headed for someplace else. A
wind full of salt was sleeping over the harbor. Old
houses, little houses, boats at anchor, lights on the
water, moon up. Sometimes you just have to be
alone—it's ordained, it must be inscribed somewhere
on a white stone. Saint Gregory of Palamas said you
can see the divine light with the eyes of your body.
I can't seem to prove it one way or another though
I'm not about to give in, even if I can't tell if I'm looking
at love or the roaming ghosts of love, or simply its
ravages. Those couples in the perfect weather for
devotion, boys and girls, boys and boys, girls and girls—
how sheltered they seemed from all the toil and risk
of the world, and yet they were moving away from
one another and from everything else, like you read
about the great drifts of the galaxies, which seem to
crave nothing but the gathering distances between
them. Maybe I am the fixed star. Maybe it's possible
to feel too much. Possible to never trace back to that
first horizon of your own ruin. But Gregory's instruction
is clear. Gaze at your own heart, he said. Watch your
own bosom rise and fall, quietly. Tell me what you see.

Sometimes I Can't Be Touched

Three bottles of water and a pot of coffee, the voices
coming in through the heavy door—kids in the passway
hailing one another—I don't listen much but I pay attention
here in the narrow room to the buzz of the fluorescent
tubes up in the suspended ceiling, stains the size
of saucers up there, brown and sad where the building
leaks once every few years. I like it here. I'm happy now
leaning into the little desk, my old fat blue bicycle leaning
too, against the wall behind me, we are practically touching
and I can reach and pluck papers and folders out of its wicker
basket, poems too. I like it, stealing these hours—every once
in a while an official knock, like a fish batting the side of a
skiff—I ignore them, they cease, it's like that, I can't be touched
or found and I can coddle my theories and stroke my evils and
blessings—oh, good days, good days, sitting, listing what I
despise, savoring what I love, plying my whole body, feeling
its torque and pressure as I try to make something turn, letting
the cheap clock tick its double-A battery down to paste—it's
like that, pushing on a heavy stone in the yard or laying your
shoulder to the back end of a stalled car while the terrified
lady with all the groceries holds on to the wheel and you try
to get her out of traffic before the light changes again—what
is it the world is trying to say to you and me? I push and push
and then there is air. I lean hard and then the clouds come. I
heave until something hurts above my left ear and then carob
trees blaze up with sullen doves—I'm getting close, I'm still
happy, I'm vanishing into all that language that isn't language,
there's less and less of me and more and more of something else,
and I can almost get to it, and I push and push, and then there
is shade and sun, and all the bricks in the courtyard offer up their

histories of clay and fire, but we're still not finished, we're still incomplete, and they come looking for me and knocking but it does them no good, and soon they leave. No one's paying attention on this side of the door. On this side of the door I'm happy. Tell them for me. Say I'm pushing on something. Say I'm hardly ever here.

Into the Second that Goes On Living

What's left of Vermeer for me. A book. Astonishing.
The remainder table in one of those horrid bookstores
that have taken over the world with people in them
who never read, so when you ask for *Crime and Punishment*
they search their machines for Sociology. But Vermeer,
that one morning, five dollars and ninety-five cents, must
I not be thankful for such grace, strong good coffee and
light coming in from the parking lot of shining cars
and shimmering on the plate glass window and lighting
the color plates, *woman, woman, woman, woman,* and
I didn't think at all of Tomas Transtromer's perfect poem,
the one that should seal away all others from Vermeer,
and so my own ignorance prevailed, jubilate and safe
for a little while, though I saw de Kooning, unwavering
in his coming-after, undaunted, *woman, woman, woman,*
and I felt that small lament, too, that there was no linseed-
smelling and high-ceilinged studio for me, full of white
light and bespattered floors and walls, thick, unguent
middens of cast-off paint, jars and cans, and sable brushes,
objects and tools I cannot define or name, but wished for,
sorry that I couldn't join this tribe of strangers for a moment,
for whom the world is light, fleshed in light, composed of it
to its very atoms, even the absence of it draping some shape
or figure in reverent darkness so that something comes through
and sits on your heart though you cannot say for a lifetime
what it is, like the necklace of small stones a man cobbles for
his lover, scooped up from the edge of the sea when the
the tide was running white-capped and blue-black, and that
she wears, in the history only, of how they gleamed once in
wave and sand, and she either doesn't notice how they have
blanched, or having seen them once radiant and transfigured—
whatever they have returned to or become—she doesn't care.

I Can See the Lapis Lazuli

Oh, the Dark Beautiful one—as though there hasn't been enough
about *him*—but it's been raining out of season and the mornings
have been even more horrible than usual, everything flat and
meaningless, every once in a while a jet flying over low looking
for the runways, and now a tall man in a cream-colored windbreaker
and matching baseball cap is slumping along the hedges, one of those
plastic grocery bags swinging from one hand, and there are little
fireflies in my head, just enough to make the darkness visible, and
of course it's all about Milton—I have been staring at that photograph
of Milton's cottage, everything sinking into me in a peculiar way, the
brickwork and the pitch of the roof, shaked and sharp, and leafy trees
the likes of which I can't name, and the grass and foxglove, and maybe
hydrangea in the foreground. And the windows—all that leadwork
binding the glass, yes, and Satan, cowled in his leathery wings, falling
for days, all that mysterious brooding, but it was Milton who knew
his heart! Milton, poking under those eaves, feeling his way around the
contours of heaven—and hell, too, because they need each other so much,
and now I can rise to my own consignment among all the hopeful and
the deluded. Marvelous angel who breaks down the distance between
evil and glory, the light is fragile, and this terrifies. The earth is wet and
smells of glory and leaves me aching between gladness and the bells of death.
So I eat the fruit. It's worth every lost soul. When we cried for more light,
what were we calling for, and to whom? Here, now, *all* the angels are dark
and beautiful, and they dance in the gardens, behind every fence and wall,
and they mean to harm me in some mysterious way that I can't refuse, that
I have somehow come to love and embrace, though the prophets warned me.
Just now, in this hour, I can see the lapis lazuli and emerald, beckoning and
dripping out in the trees. Yes, something is lovely there, something better
than my own gloom, and I can't keep myself from walking through that door.

Black Notebook # 1, Gideon Bible, Los Angeles

The fire already over the peaks of the houses, the light going from them in the street's gloaming hour, the dread sublime, the columns of smoke as from a furnace, the fire in the sky with its double stars and hidden birds, the fire of the lone duck beating low over the wires of the city, the thunder in the mountains, the howling along the freeways, the trash wedged in the chainlink, beercans, condoms, plastic bags, all the small fires thereby, amaryllis, trumpet-vine, lavender, acanthus, the twisted limbs of the sycamores, fire in the Mexican sage, silent fire, ravening fire, devouring, in the letter of a friend, still considering: the fire of *Angels or no Angels?* The same friend: *Love saves the soul in fire, and you know it,* the fire of the unknowable, the fire of the daughters, the fire of their wine in the throats of all the fathers, the fire of their love and the fire of their truth, the fire of the fathers, the fire in the fathers' seed, the sons marching, the scarlet banners and the black banners, the ash and the pitch hailing down, war our whole lives long, the city trembling beneath the squealing tires of the long trucks, their wheels of riot, their wheels of fire, their rumble, the fire of the heart, the fire in the heart, the pillar of salt, its lick on the tongue, the faces in the windows, the bodies at the doors, the fire in the eyes that watched, *Angels or no angels,* how they came forth naked and walked in the streets, the two together in the long snows of fire, how they came to my door and banged on its brass, fire in their earthly splendor, fire as I bid them enter, fire in their eyes as they knew me, and then my own fire, the everlasting fire they had come for.

The Lesser Alleluia

This is for when you have been proven and receive the crown of life.
It differs from the *Greater Alleluia,* for the *Greater* includes a robe
of glory, *stolam gloriae.* You tally up your mistakes and miscalculations
which are many, no doubt, and there is an accounting—there would
have to be, for what is to be made in the defense of all your languors
and sashays and wastes and vanities? Who can say? The wind is up
from the harbor full of fish and diesel and it makes a kind of crown,
it certainly makes the maples flush and reach and shake like the woman
I just met rushing to meet her lover, feet in the earth, but, oh, the wild
look in her eye, such resolve, her hair unfurling, irrepressible Magdalene,
won't she be redeemed over and over, all day long? All the Buddhas
smile. You might be one of them. I can't keep track of all the kingdoms,
poor Hagar weeping until the angel comes, but he doesn't give her too
much—or maybe he does: Ishmael and the wild people. Let's be sober
for just a minute amongst all the shining opals and jaspers of this one
day. Let's consider this *Alleluia.* The small one. The crown of life.
I think you wear it. I think it speaks for itself, it cries out of every
breath, an enduring thank you, a vaulting praise whether you know it
or not. How can it be otherwise? Would you change Hagar's story?
Would you nudge that woman from her ecstatic path with the wind
in her hair? You wouldn't if you could, which of course you can't.
For myself, I'll choose the small one, the *Lesser.* I must have decided
a long time ago. Every time I look, it's what I witness and what I seal.
I wear it like a crown, I suppose you could put it that way, you could
say that, even though I can't claim to renounce all the temptations
and their worldly beauties. In fact, I seem to follow them, I rush
after them, too, around so many corners and along all the cobbled
streets that run only in one direction but that seem to get you where
you want to go, sooner or later. Down to the tall ships that bear you
away to Nineva and Tyre or the casual delights of Cordova. Oh, where

is that woman now, pulled by the blood's gravities? Let's praise something about her, living creature under the laws, unfathomable. Let's commend that she lives and craves, her fleeting happiness, her wild weeping, when it comes, as it surely will. It's all exactly right. *Alleluia*.

I Changed My Clothes with a Beggar Once

—Saint Francis speaks

I love beauty—I admit it—I loved the beauty of the sick and
the dying. God speaks through me. This is true, but God speaks
through everyone. That's why all the confusion. Women are more
beautiful than young girls, but the young girls are beautiful and make
me sad for death and all my blunders of the spirit. I adored Clare
and adore her still. She adored me. We did the best we could. God
gave us free will. God is complete freedom within His own bounds.
You can think about that for a while. Once I thought I wanted my
heart to grow until the world would sit inside it like a bright egg.
This was a blunder of the spirit, for what could the stars, so azure
and distant have to do with Clare and her naked feet? Everything,
of course, but what living man wants such a fusion in his head?
An ordinary fool. Better to dash your heart on black stones than to keep
it full and whole. Better to shatter the windows and burn the doors.
Then the wind will come up from the meadows and the smell of hay.
Birds and moths will fly through, blue and orange, and the little beasts
of the forest. And men and women and their loveliness will pass by
like the shadows of the clouds. You will be empty. You will be nothing.

Black Notebook #5, Lisbon

Where sleep kept itself across the room like a long sheet
of glass, and he lay on the white bed sifting through the ash
and raking over the cinders of one burned-out dream or
another, as if he would ever find a shy feather from the angel's
wing there, no sweet or bitter powder to stop all the circling
in his head, all that grinding over and over, yielding up nothing,
and down in the street some marvelous and bejeweled girls
calling out to one another, and car doors slamming outside
the trendy club with its drift of icy music. They had gone looking
for Pessoa and found him on coffee mugs and tee shirts, they had
gone singing for Eça and Florbela and found cobblestones and
tiled walls and the bayonet rails of the crimson trolleys. How
far will any voyage take you? You can follow Roget and see how
the slap is the first glance toward murder. You can misread
the physicists and believe that hope and despair are the same
string vibrating. Love what you will quickly. You can never
stay. Deliverance never looks like itself. Weary and homeward,
then, outbound, the hard-won tickets, and the baggage groaning
with holy books in every language, the great Atlantic cloud cover,
glacial and complete, showed the curvature of the round earth and
they all wept in at least one of the rooms of the heart, for they were
all leaving *something,* each of them, unguessable and sovereign in
the deepest vault, or profound in those arcane inner whirlwinds
of marvel and fatigue. How much later then, in his little canted
rooms, home, still with the delicacies and caresses of his own
descent in the November sun. Now the nodding maple crowning
in his high windows, boughs pressing in on him, like the nose of a
lost cat against a door, all hope and resolve that the house and its
joys will open. In that moment of common fusion he saw himself
reaching through the windowpane and petting its leaves, already
cold and mortal, and the south-facing limbs easing into their final

rusts and crimsons. As if he could pass through anything, he put out his hand but then only laid the flat of it against the glass. It was deeply cool, surprising in the drench of westering light, and he left his palm there for a while against a billion molecules, once opaque and blind but now because they had joined in fire he could look through them clearly as if through one single bright jewel, and he believed in this way he could see many pieces of the scattered world.

The Marriage of Figaro

There were music books, which we couldn't keep or take home
or hide in our lockers. We opened them on our laps as we sat in
the folding chairs. We handed them back, after, so that the others who
came behind us could open them on *their* laps. Eight years of school
and we still pronounced *Mozart* wrong. I can still be the boy now,
even in those shameful moments when all I want to do is disavow him,
the one with the holes in his shoes, for which he inserted cardboard,
which worked well enough except for when winter came, the rain
and slush, how in music period in the overheated auditorium the foot
would not un-numb, the sock would not dry, having wicked up the weather
into so many small humiliations and miseries. There was a piano in the corner,
and secret places behind the stage, up ladders, everywhere, but when your
mind is in your wet shoe it tends to stay there. Now, in the new millennium,
I make a tuna sandwich at one a.m. I drink a beer. The terror of so many
notebooks with nothing to fill them with but these weird intimations. Blue
stars on the roof, barking and hammering. The multitudinous names of god
cutting loose from the branches when the wind threshes the yard. All my
last chances in brilliant drag, rolling by in a slow parade, blowing kisses
and tossing beads. This is what it comes to sometimes, and then I will darken
the house so that I can't tell the cat from a typewriter or any of the other
small knobs and shadows. Then it gets just right. I can say the world is at rest,
and there's no one to dispute it. I can say time has stopped, but every vague
noise is an increment on somebody's mortal clock. It makes no difference.
I can sit and try to remember then—like trying to trace an old melody
that you heard once and that moved your heart, but you can't quite begin
to hear it again in your head—try to remember what it was exactly—
maybe a thing that happened a long time ago, when all the stars were dust,
and you and I were nothing among the long galleries of nothingness, and
then came Mozart and a hole in my shoe, and all our little voices trying to sing.

Hart Crane, Black Notebook #2, Los Angeles

Am *I* the prodigal then, pushed from the door, unloved? Are you
talking to *me,* frail and fickle in all my creeds and philosophies,
sailor you would have loved? Followed? Me, skinny in bellbottoms,
sitting at the long gray daytime bars with the weary bargirls, so lost
and hopeless all of them, but something about them that made
their slow drowning so comely and fierce? *How many dawns?*
How many aching dawns to endure, rising to nothing but the noise
of the world, when all I want is someone to talk to over coffee and
make my life mean something for a few minutes. There are crickets
tonight, October, it has rained and then an unseemly heat has
settled upon us. There are lights in the sky. The street is so quiet
that you can be fooled into thinking you hear the wind, but I believe
it's a great electrical hum all around us, and it alerts me to a kind
of comfort I am not quick to trust. I am trying to twist and turn
something. I trespass freely and allow myself these little forays
into the harbors of death. The hawsers are chafing in their iron
cleats, Saint Elmo's fire in the rigging. We're all at sea. I remember
my own long ship heaving with power and grace, the bow in a languid
pitch into the green running hills of water, and the flying fish in
their multiple hundreds rising as one carpet and gliding over the
ocean, black and yellow in breathless flight. This was in youth with
all the mysteries before me and the sky all fraught with the streak
of bombs, and then the compassionate stars, you could take your
pick between them. So then. Mortal and unshackled we made our
way. We will never meet. I can't think of any wages allowed for
talking to the dead. Union card. Seaman's papers. From the rail
of the *Orizaba,* 275 miles north of Havana, 10 miles east of Florida,
I know who *you* are. Me, I'm the one standing under the lamp on
that narrow street that runs along the foot of the pier. It's a bit too
familiar, the fog rolling along like smoke and me in my pea-coat with

the big collar up and a cigarette in my lips. I'm watching for something. That lamp and that fog make a faint globe of light above my head. It's a big world. I doubt if anyone will ever notice me here.

I Wash the Buddha

When you walk out the other side of all those little fires
in your life, when you burrow up from all those petty graves
people are forever trying to seal you away in, your eyes
always get a little dimmer, but yet they shine a light in a way
that they didn't before. You see things for what they aren't,
and the splendors start adding up. I tell myself the truth, that
I didn't gouge the heart from the songs, I didn't suck the soul
from the poems, I didn't fill the air with the withering noise
of the lying voices. It's enough to sweat in the summer night
and leave the delicacy of my fingerprints on the cheap paper
of my old copy of the *Flowers of Evil,* where they will remain
like shy ghosts until the book itself is no longer. Or to trim
the hydrangea, not knowing where exactly to cut beneath
the blown purple. Then I water the clay pots, I wash the
Buddha and the porch, the miracle of the hose, which rains
wherever I bid it. And the Buddha himself who said that
suffering is the great disease of the world, that I must stop
the turning of my mind. Bliss is not divine, but human. *If
only.* Then the teachings start. I'm not equal to them. I'm
drawn to the little flames, the little furrows in the earth where
I so often am seduced to lie down. I don't struggle. You might
even say it becomes me, this misbegottenness. When I watch
the blue morning glories follow the sun with their shameful kisses,
I really believe I understand their yearnings. And the spiritual
loneliness of the honeybees in all their rumble and crowding.
And when the marauding raccoon comes vandalizing my
fountain to steal the little screens from the filter, I'm
fine with it. I just watch through the window with some
poems in my lap. Truthfully, sometimes I think she's me.

The Wild Swans

They went out to look at the wild swans. They walked in silence
through oak and heather, but those names might not be correct.
The woods glowed, though the sun was yellow, and buttered
the leaves and branches with its yellowness. Light everywhere
and then the pond, glistening smooth like the tear over an eye.
They watched there, and the swans, after all, became geese,
bullish and noisy and black on the black pond. All the sadness
of the world is here now, he thought, but that was just his old
malady talking. All the peace of the world is here now, he thought
and let it stand, because the wind for a moment came, and shushed
all through the trees, and not a ripple rose on the pond, flat as iron
and fat in the distance with its magic geese. Then they sat apart
for a while. There was a chill to the air and it was pleasant to feel.
Every now and then the geese, too far away to count or distinguish,
would rise up and roar at the woods and settle again into their darkness.
Who isn't a well of secrets? Who can reckon himself completely? Let
the heart inhabit the heart. Let the mind inhabit the mind. Let the leaves
shiver all around the ferocious mouths of those wild birds. How deep
they had walked into the quiet, how far away, how alone, even when
the swans turned into geese, even while the yellow sun laved the forest.

When You Saw the Lightning

When I was a fish—in that time when no one
walked the long tangled banks of the pond in
those deep woods unscarred by roads—oh, you should
have seen me, my long fish body one muscle, and
my will narrowed to the fine essentials! You would
have cried out for my beauty when I leapt into the
sun and air and you saw the rainbows and lightning
on my stippled back. And I would have made *you*
jump. Your breath would have caught above your
heart, and you would have loved me in that certain
way that we love things beyond any need for them,
but desiring them senselessly. Yes, the buzz of the
dragonflies, and then my killing heart in the shade
of the lilies, in the black water with all its treasures,
and my wicked teeth, and how the green leaves on
the trees shuddered when I rose and struck! That was
when I was a fish. I would never lie to you about that.
I don't know why I would tell you this now. I don't
know why you would even listen to anything in a poem
except that it might stop you for a moment, it might
make you lift your head and look around in just that
lonely hour of the day or night when the world isn't
quite enough. Oh, yes, I was a power—I razed that
hidden world with splendor and terror, and if you
only could have seen me, your breast would have been
filled with rapture, I'm sure of it. Along those wild
shores, along that gloss of water, among the sweet
greens of summer—where were you?

Pond

When he left, and when he was finally gone, he thought he was nothing on this earth, though there was no *he* and no *thought,* and he believed he would join the vast armies of the dead that he had heard about, but nothing flew up through his breast and nothing raised up from him. Then the woman held him in a wooden box, and he heard her say how it was heavy, so heavy, and that it was mostly crushed bone among the black ashes. Her hands were strong. They were always busy, and he had always admired them, but they were both beyond that now. She shook him gently from the box at some point. It was what they knew as *morning.* She always liked to hear the coffee coming down, the burbling noise it made in the white machine on her kitchen counter. She shook him into a paper sack and put a smooth stone from the beach into it. Their minds had been alike in some ways. There was a good weight to the stone. He knew it. They had picked it out together. It was the size of her heart. Then she carried him. She walked the path out through the woods and to the pond. She wore what they once called sneakers and denim pants, a wool sweater. When they reached the shore, she stepped into the water, which was like the sky at night, black and shining, and she walked out until the water was near to her shoulders, and her breath blew and shuddered. Then she let him go. It was everything they had hoped for, in those times they had hoped. He went down. He settled. He might have lain immured in the sack for weeks. It was a surprise. He loved the cold water and he loved it more as it ate of the sack until it no longer was, as he no longer was, and without a way to tell it clearly, he slowly became the pond, spreading with the slowest, quietest eddies. So slow. He could not say where he had been, or what. But when the ice came, he was the ice and at the same time he saw up through its gray ceiling, and he saw more gray. Snow came then, a dusty white, like clouds, and then it thickened and he was everywhere under a black quilt, moving, as nothing moved. When the summer sun came he was in the fish and the fish were in him. When the lilies rose, he rose in their veins, and when they bloomed white and impure, he was in their throats, and they made a broken kind of singing. When the stars drifted over, the frogs roared. Then there was a kind of laughter. This is all a way of speaking when there is truly no speaking. He didn't know where the others were, but it would be wrong to think that anything was the same, that there were desires or feelings, or even *others*. After a while *everything* and *nothing* were just sounds the living made, he barely knew them. If there were speech, he would say just one thing: Your realm above the glassed eye of this silent water is just a dream. This other place, this forever, this forgetting— this, always, was the only world.

Three

Unable to Amend My Life I Began Another Book

Some days I would walk in the late afternoon
out among the barrel cactus and cholla gardens,
when the light was finally growing weak enough to be
caught among the spines and needles and suffer there.
Yahweh was in all the ridges, sharp as a chalk line,
bluing the dusk. Silent. Fierce. Then I was like a glove
turned inside out, how it becomes the other hand. Then
it was possible that God did not understand man or woman,
only His own purposes. I had to ignore the traces and evidence.
They were too terrible. I had to make up my own reasons for
everything, for how I felt when the heat went out of the land
when the sun dipped behind the shoulders of the earth. I had
to invent the whirlwind and the coyote. I tried, in this case, to
put it all down in long strings of characters. Sometimes, late
in the night, sweating through my skin, I would watch the language
crawl forth without me, always in the same direction. Then
I thought there might not be enough words or letters, for the script
itself became a thing. For it took on its own purpose. I couldn't
divine what it was. Then I made it so the blood of the covenant
never spattered on the desert floor. So there was never an ache
among the cool aisles of soda and beer in the highway's convenience
market. But it all felt wrong. I had no idea what time it was by then,
but it was black outside. The sky was gone. There were some tiny lights
in the farthest distance, where I thought the horizon should be.
A town, perhaps. And people in it. Lives. But I knew I would
never understand them. It would all have to be fixed. I couldn't
any longer be the same man trapped inside the same man.
I would have to work it out. I took up the long pencils.
I labored for hours. Maybe it was days. When I finally turned off
the air conditioner for a few moments of silence, I could hear

a bird of some kind, a cry like an arrow shrieking. Behind that
I heard big-rigs moaning up the Interstate, though it was five miles away.
They sounded like wind. I didn't open the heavy drapes, but I could
sense the daylight behind them. That white heat. That enormous weight.

Are We Not Safe Here?

There is something very strange now about the wars,
how they seem to go on and on all by themselves, whether
anyone's tending them or not. None of our roofs are flying
the black flags—all the smoke must be in somebody else's sky.
Often at night I hear the groan of an airplane under the stars,
but nobody here mistakes it for the angel of death. Mostly
the summer nights on our street shine darkly, like mother
of pearl, and the moon is aloof and stunning—it surprises me
and stops me in my tracks, and I end up gazing and thinking
of gold and steel or some other kind of alchemy. That's what
I'm doing out on the curb. Something is shimmering. This
search for the one pure element. Two or three houses down
a light comes on, smooth and hypnotic beneath the relentless
whirl of the constellations. After a time it goes off again.
Josephus Flavius, Jew and then Roman, who mentions the word
Jesus just twice, obliquely, in his massive history of the wars
in Judea, once invited a group of elders he disagreed with
to his house to eat dinner and to negotiate. When they arrived
his men beat them with scourges until their organs oozed from
their flayed skin. Then he threw them into the street. But
all in all he was said to have been a thoughtful man. I'm trying
to take this all in. Maybe he knew why Moses struck the rock
or why Aaron lifted his rod. A general of the Hebrew army, he
admired the Roman legions and their short swords and their
intelligent cruelty. Maybe that's why he went over to them
after a while. It is what it is. That light, on and then off, down
the street. What is *that?* Are we not safe here? Maybe someone
has risen from the shrouds of sleep to shuffle into the kitchen for
a sandwich and then be born again. Maybe somebody dreamed
she walked to the edge of the lake of blood and back. I can't

assemble the proper cadences to capture the moment—why
I have left my own lamp and my own kitchen and my own books.
But I stay out in the night air for awhile, the mild tang of the Pacific,
the big-armed trees. Josephus, being long dead, will wait. His old
dusty wars will wait. His readers will continue to argue about Jesus.
We are ignorant and fearful. You must try to understand us.

There Are Three Heavens

I was working my way down to Tallahassee, where I thought
I could put my suitcase down and be safe for a while even though
there are snakes and alligators there and crazy birds that will peck
your heart out if you're not wise to them. There are *good* snakes too,
and bluebirds, and birds that dive for fish, and birds that sing and
gorge all the dripping foliage with blooms of color, and there are
rickety stands along the roads where you can buy fruit and woven
baskets to put it in, and yellow corn, if I remember that right. You
can take little highways down from the north, so many good roads
to choose from. Your burdens—you can roll them in a canvas tarp
and tie them up on the roofrack, and all the other pilgrims can see
them for what they are—just a limp roll of junk on the top of your
dusty car, and they will salute you with a small nod or a little pucker
of their lips while they motor by you on the hot blacktop, and you
will nod and purse your lips too, you will see their baggage and their
luggage, and you will never learn the exact nature of their sorrows,
and you would never say any of you are defiled or depraved, but you
are all in this together, like that family today in the old panel truck.
We had slept in the same turnout, and in the dark of the morning
the young daughter came over, shining with the jumper cables, and
asked for a start off my battery and I obliged, happy to serve. She was
so pale and white, with her dark hair pulled back, and red sneakers,
and her smile was better than the sunrise, because according to certain
texts I had been reading she might be an angel, and then I might be an angel
too, because I put my drift and confusion aside for the moment, and then
the sun only blared into my left front window when I finally headed down
the two-lane, puzzling about all my choices and whether or not I would
be delivered. There was still time to catch 221 out of Georgia to the 146
coming in from the east, or maybe swinging over to the 53, down Alabama,
and then there was the 111, the 112, the 122, and who knows what other

secrets and revelations. Then I had time to think about how it would be when I got there, some good poets and plenty of books and guitars, beer and smoked mullet, and dark pools among the twisted tree limbs weeping with moss and the air thick with butterflies and cicadas. I thought maybe then the weight on me would lift for a while and rise like swift clouds into grandeur and purity. Maybe I would even sing some songs there. Nights would be lush with sleep, and I would lay my spinning head down, and then I would be refreshed and made new, and sooner or later I would awaken in that green, sweet-smelling garden, and I would begin to dream again.

Black Notebook, Day Six, Canadian Rockies

One Bighorn, fifteen female elk, marmots, an enormous fox, the size of a dog, glorious, red, bristling, hunting. Hiking Edith Cavell trail up to Glacier, some cold rain, then clearing out across the ice fields, a slow reveal, sky bluing darkly then bright sun, mountain, dream-walls, cirques, the astonishment of the scale here, the brilliant brooding blue vascular seethe of ice over rock earth, you'd think a burden, a weight, grinding, but even here where the simplest of molecules hold tight to themselves without sense or mind, as we are told, there is this rubbing and yielding this give and take, go and come of making and changing, birth, death, the slow ecstasies of friction, the quarrying, the sliding. Edith Cavell, Edith Cavell. Where will we find her? Dead of course, and living forever maybe, her name up on the ice, the enduring granite, Nurse in the *Great War*. The way they talk about war, how David slew so and so, and Joshua blew down a wall, and all the daughters of Israel weeping by the waters of Babylon and pledging to dash the brains from the children of their enemies. Edith Cavell nursed everyone. She made no distinction among them, no enemies, no foes, just young boys, the age of my son or your daughter, or the age of me when I sailed with the ships of death to the walls of Troy and Carthage, it doesn't matter, it never stops. German, French, English. She held them, wrapped them, bound wounds and gave comfort, and watched them die when there was nothing else she could do. But she helped *all* of them. And then she began helping her lovely doomed boys escape the war. She hid them. She led them to safe houses. When her station was overrun, for her unbound compassion she was imprisoned, tried and shot to death. This will either be a poem or it will be something else. From here you can see a smudge in the sky far off, the shadow of a cloud and the dark catenary scarf beneath that is rain falling again, but out beyond the great blue fields yet. Maybe it's altitude, this sharp tang in the lungs, the rhythmic breathing that matches each footfall, the slow building ache in the top of the thighs. When the wind punches freezing across the ice you understand that you can only go so far. You have to get back down before the night ever comes.

White Chair, Moonlight, Three A.M.

Then the moon was gibbous and waxing, just a few days short
of full, and it drifted behind the house to the west, and so its light
became the color of clear water tumbling from a fountain, and it
fell like a haze upon the high barricade of the camphor trees,
and then onto the lawn, and the white chair and the white
daisies, the chair solitary with the cloaked lawn beneath. It had
nothing to say except in its language of *light-among-shadow*,
which was silent and puzzling, and so it arrested him, it held him
behind his kitchen window for long minutes, and in that quiet
he slid into the world of objects and became lost among their
lost souls and their own bewilderment—and he was taken up, too
with their open hands and their pure expressions. Then he knew
he could walk among them and sift through their paling shapes,
a thing among things, and he could be touched by their sameness
which would become his own in this obscure hour, when the
refrigerator churned among the faucets and the canisters, and there
appeared in the black window the indistinct shape of a man who
was barely reflected, who moved when *he* moved and who was still when
he was still, who had strayed like a ghost between the dark and the silver.

Sometimes a Light Shines on a Book

It's a terrible thing to be trapped in a particular mode of expression. You have to struggle every day, and for every inch you don't gain you are visited with a disaster. True, they are small damages, but they add up. You feel the mathematics in your knees or in the bones of your spine, or worse. Early this morning the sun was shining on the bookstand over in the little park by the library, and there, waiting specifically for my hand was Thucydides. Seventy-five cents. The Thomas Hobbes translation, seventeenth-century English. It looked like it had never been opened, but you can hardly blame anyone for that. War and more war. It must be inside of me. It's everywhere, and it's the only explanation. All day, all day, in the blue chair, sun over my shoulder. Those Athenians, self-righteous cruel pricks jerking the Melians around and explaining that they had the right to do so because justice means nothing in the face of raw power. The Melians pleaded. Then they fought. Then they surrendered. *The Athenians thereupon put to death all who were of military age, and made slaves of the women and children.* It was almost like reading yesterday's newspaper. Later I went walking in the mall, and Thucydides was in my head, or maybe it was Hobbes and his horrid and elegant prose. Everyone there marched in a certain ghostly rhythm, past the stores and jewelry carts, the wallets and cell phones. Men in checkered shorts and sandals. Women in almost anything you could name. Kids cloaked in their own private unreadable worlds. I could see the burdens of love grinding on the bodies. Or I could see the dull terrors of *no* love grinding on the bodies, but the two are not the same. Maybe it's correct, this idea that the world is an endless billow of sentences, all true in the flash of the moment, and then all lies ever after. Think about the gorgeous marble torsos and columns of Athens. Aphrodite, Hera, Apollo. Beauty, we say. Art. What is left? By then I had already fallen into step with the others. I was gazing at their faces in that garish heaven of air-conditioning and eternal drifting music. I was already choosing those among them I would adore.

New Translations

Certainly you were the prophet we were all waiting for,
sitting up in the obscure hours with your battered
notebooks on your lap, counting the vowels in the poems
of the Rose of Sharon or the gospels of Mary Magdalene.
How lonely you felt when the angels finally never marched
down your street playing their tambourines and samba drums,
calling out to you, how a little nail stuck at the back of your
throat because they never clamored for you to be raised up.
All that exile. A year's worth of bottles and cans carted out to
the state recycling barn for the deposit money, and the piles
of newspapers making canyons in your damp little rooms, holding
the sacred light there. Maybe you are the absolute shadow of me.
All over the city I can hear the vows being broken. Everyone
I meet in this world hands me a mask, and I either try it on
or I burn it straight away. After all, don't we, all of us, think
we are the dark mysterious thing in the rock waiting for the right
sword to strike us into holy fire? Do I have it right? Maybe I am
someone else tonight, some particular glimmer come into the
room without explanation or cause. Now I am banging my head
against a book of ancient psalms, my new translations, so dense
and melancholy, so beautiful in the their hollow-voiced recitatives.
The trees on my street are bare-limbed and dark against the sky.
When I lie back on the old couch and stare out the window for a
while, they no longer look like trees. They look like foreign shapes,
twisted and frightening, like the wild arms of someone raving.

The Edge, Black Notebook #10, Desert Queen Motel

He wrote that the militias were killing the bus drivers
because they picked up boys and girls and rode them together
in the same vans. Because they drove girls to school, some of
the girls with their heads uncovered. Then he wrote that in
America hundreds of earnest poets were writing about sorrow
and lilacs. He knew it was no use. Then he wrote about the war,
the old one that he had gone to, but it bored him and so it would
bore the reader. It occurred to him, not for the first time, that
the normal mind would not let him live in such deprivation. He
considered the growing disorder of the room. He decided he would
finally let the maids enter the next time they knocked. Towels. Sheets.
Their coffee uniforms and coffee skin. What kept them in such
a place? They smiled at his language, but there was so much trouble
in their eyes. A hundred and two at four in the afternoon. A haze
over the ridges. On a day when the power stuttered and everything
died briefly and then came back and he lost several pages in the
machine despite following all the protocols. Apples and chocolate
on the bureau, a shard of quartz he had found. Now his brother
was dead, but he kept going. Love was out of the question, and
he didn't despair over that. All that about love, like the color of
one's hair, or if your teeth came in straight. He'd settled into what
he was and what he was not. No surprises anymore. Where was
the abode of love in that larger place? Which heart mattered?
He ate without ceremony, or he did not eat. He wanted an angel.
He had wanted one for a long time. Perhaps thus the desert.
He weighed one hand against the other. He labored and made
a place for both the quartz and the chocolate. He labored over
the lost pages, how they seemed so correct now that they were gone
and how the new attempts would not rise to his memory of what
had been. And the angel. The angel. He began about the angel.
And the maids came knocking on the heavy door, calling out to him.

Do No Harm

Already I am waiting for spring and all the little annunciations
—waiting for the moral fog to lift and for something better
to shine through. There is not a single thing I'm innocent of,
and this comes as a great disappointment to me. I was watching
the boys and girls today, the way they strolled the docks and
parkways, their backpacks, their earphones, the gray light striking
their wild hair and eyes, the way they circled each other, each other's
hearts betraying them to darker purposes. It's always the same story,
the broken find each other, the broken believe they will mend each other.
Someone should put a stop to it. The sea is already full of tears
according to everything I've read about it. Then I look at my winter yard
in all its browns and reds, the myrtle trees like forlorn sticks,
who would think there was life inside? And the bare ivy clinging
black to the wall like death itself. All this used to make sense.
Now I am reading a book that tells me every raindrop falls to earth
exactly as it's supposed to. That there are no errors. Therefore,
there is no *therefore*. Nothing to do then except to go out to
the porch and listen to the birdsong, listen to the prevailing
wind up in the leafless branches. Do no harm, I told myself.
Look for the small miracles. Already the moon was crisp in the east.
Already the moon was faultless behind the naked limbs, following
the black notes of the huddled birds, shining, and it wasn't even dark yet.

You Can Hear It

Puccini, late, late, the earphones warm on my skin
and one cat against my bare leg, and one curled, just
a soft touch at the back of my wrist. My heart is broken
perpetually. It's all a quandary of errors. I am equal
to nothing. How, I ask myself, will I ever manage to
pull a sound from my own body after five minutes and
fourteen seconds of *Sono Andati,* which I can't even
understand any better than my own chronic soul and
its unending wars and armistices. I, who have not wept
aloud for my own losses, now sob quietly for what I
know is coming—*O Dio, Mimi.* Can we not agree to
spare her life for just once? It's an altered state. I don't
repent of it yet, either. If death frames all beauty and
beauties, tell me then—why are we not in one another's
arms in every breathing moment before that blood earth
drinks us up again? Here's when the horns come in—
that crescendo—and the violins and then something else.
I don't know what it is—it would be ridiculous to care at
this moment. And then—I love this even as I know it will
kill any hope of sleep for the night—the almost silent
hiss from the ancient recording caught there in the fuzz
of ones and zeros. The almost-silence that stands for
nothing. You can hear it. We have to save somebody.

Myrtle

When she began the long fade. When she lay, forgetting everything.
When she lightened in the bright days and her only words
became small rumors in her throat, and their meanings crept
and hid from her as the prophets always said they would, then
I took up the books and I found *The Fire in the Lake,* and *That which
lets now the dark, now the light appear.* I found *He hides his weapons
in the thicket,* and *The Seven Thunders.* I found *The Pillars of Fire*
and *The Mighty Angel with The Rainbow on his Head.* That was
when she became smaller and smaller and fumbled my name among
the lush wastes of nothing. It was during that fall when whole
kingdoms were also dying. It was when, in the cradle of my yard, the green
dragonflies came to shine. And then the monarchs and the swallowtails.
And mourning doves. And the mockingbirds. And the ravening bees.
The crepe myrtles, too, had begun their changes. Heavy and abundant,
the blossoms, blown and brazen, pink and purple, drooping in bushels, weary
amid their own crowns, the slender limbs bent to earth by their burdens.
The bees made a trembling in the air. And those transfigured trees.
What could they have ever meant to me then, there, after the thunder and
the fire, the light and the dark, and the vanished kingdoms of the earth?
When the glutting bees crowded the death-sweet flowers and wallowed
in their frowsy sugars, and reeled and swooned in the death-sweetness?

I Piece Things Together

I take a little milk and honey every now and then,
not from anybody's holy book, just from my own kitchen,
soymilk, sometimes, warmed in the microwave late at night
when the rest of the world seems asleep, though the cats
and I know that's just an illusion. The rains are here again
and I can sit in the darkened room at the front of the house
and watch the street, the orange lamps on their high poles,
the neighbors' porch lights, here and there a window lit,
never a rolling car at this hour, never a man's or a woman's
shadow moving black against the black. Now I can take a little
Blake and the Gospel of James, I can take a sip from the golden cup.
One cat sits on the chair back, one at the edge of the rug. They
watch the street. They are vigilant. How subtly their sharp ears
move and adjust, how fierce they gaze at all the dangers and all
they would maul and destroy except that it lies on the other side
of the bay window. Then I take a little whiskey and a little water
for my lavish inner life and its nine circles of hell, I take a little
white pill or two for the holy ghost and its promise of rapture.
All day I balance the body and soul as one. The pieces do not
lie easily together. All night they sunder themselves and leave
one another keening in their loneliness. It's not my fault. I'm
the one who rises and keeps watch with my animals. I'm the
one who was chosen. I take a little air, I take a few heartbeats,
I take the rain and the way it slants down, I take the black lines
of the trees, I do what I can, I piece things together, whatever fits.
It's not much. This is the only sort of thing I can make out of it.

Black Notebook #7, Desert Queen Motel

Was it death he fell out of then, that long nothing before life,
that emptiness broken as with a ripple on a tear, one divisor
in all that eternity—how sometimes raving he thought he came
here by a tortuous shift of his own will and not purely some
unbidden and random desire on the part of others before him?
And now, to not make a sound—that is, to not issue voice from
his body. He went out on the black highway to the little sagging
store. Roiling heat. He bought some things for the room—whisky,
bread, jam, peanut butter, sliced meats. He did not have to say
those words, but to exchange pleasantries with the gold-haired
watchful woman at the checkstand, how nice the day was, and
thank you. One hundred and four degrees in these particular
latitudes of the ether. The desert red as iron. There was no room
for error. The crucible, the mortar, the forge. Everywhere was
cruelty and judgment. Nothing would last. Hard edges. Slag and
ivory, down the walled canyon into the crusts, the old stamp
mills and shafts, their timbers muscular even in their desiccation
and ruin, their mordant lagging into the earth, and by them
yet ran the dry washes, undulate, mounding, cleft and open
among towering stone. Back in the room he could work at the table
with his shirt off. He could lie on the bed naked. A box of books. A box
of paper. Then days and days without speech, without presence,
except those voices on the page, which rose from nothing, in un-
civil announcements. The ascent into a kind of madness which
he loved and which love he had learned to dread. The endless work,
which was a lie, for it would end. Picture the Elohim meeting at a
long table, so mysterious there is no way to speak of them in
his present language. Here where there should be only nothing.
Not angels but the flame of the angels' swords. Splendor and
disaster. The withholding towers of cloud, pendulous and always
distant, the nights sheared by the wheel-saw of the zodiac. Black

constellations in his own eyes that he had not noticed before, hours
during which all the machines stroked and shuddered and the lamps
quailed. That afternoon his path was blocked by a rattlesnake
coiled plentifully in the blare of the sun. He sat simply, closely,
and let the precision of its markings hold him still. Then later
repeating again at the table, *this is life, I have fallen here from death,
here, into a place where there should be nothing.* Somewhere
along the narrow hallway of doors a man and a woman argued
in Spanish. Long into the night. The woman wept. Keened. Wailed.
They became a fountain of broken syllables. His own walls, the heat
breathing from them, the sweet ends of bread, the rinds of cheese.
At some point he would break open. Then he would let everything in.

September 10th—Black Notebook, Unnumbered

I was sitting up on the graves in Provincetown, my back against the old *Gaspar* stone, and I could feel my grandfather angry and restless and hating to be dead. He wanted to laugh and walk along the wharves and streets and be greeted and hailed and loved, and drink cheap wine again. I should have brought that *other* stone with me, the black lava rock from Pico Azores that I plucked from the beach outside of what is maybe the little village that all the old ones harbored from, how I could push it into the sandy earth and cover it over and something at last would be *done*. One day I will bear it here. Another day I will fall here like blown dust. I took a bottle of green wine and opened it and poured some out and let it sink into the ground. Then I drank some, and then I poured some more on the graves, like that, back and forth, and I talked out loud to the dead, some going back so far I knew almost nothing about them but had only the gravure on the weathered granite to steer by. Sometimes to get to the new Eden you have to step on the head of the dragon. That much was written somewhere. All these gardens and forests of death. So beautiful in the light. Light everywhere and the old stones gleaming over the burying fields, white and gray, little tufts of spiky grass nestled here and there. What is the moral order of stone that it has so much to do with how love never knows where its limits are or when to stop in this world with all its perennial Gomorrahs and Jerusalems wedged flagless in the heart? Your heart and mine. Do you dream? Do you ever hear the sea? Are you broken? Are you whole and upright? The women here love God every day in their long garments, and lean over the white fences eternally and whisper to one another. The men are all hoarse and sinewy and hard at work. Somewhere in the Atlantic of mysteries it is snowing, and they are in the boat, long and narrow, heaving and shouting at the oars. The distance closes, they are making way. When I hear them, I *hear* them, but I don't know all the words. The snow aslant, the ocean fierce and peaked and black. Yet there are no impediments to their perpetual coming. By one oarlock, an empty space on the thwart. Laid along the freeboard a single clean oar. One day I will bruise my head. Another day I will bruise my heel.

The Secret Book of John

The days have shortened, and the leaves are dying into their weariest colors and shiver and turn their bellies up to the wind. Soon the angels will usher them from the garden, or so one might say—so *I* might say, lying under the fan that mows the air now that an errant heat has returned for a single day against all gist of season. I am naked with *The Secret Book of John*, deep in the Gnostic Heresies, where Yahweh is the miscarried broken one, dark and jealous and incomplete. It makes so much sense. Nothing is our fault. He is to blame for this shattered world and our tattered natures. It's late, and I can have anything I want, a bowl of peaches, or a cup of gin. When I stepped into the tiny kitchen earlier, I banged my head again against the low eave, and then a fat mouse startled and ran waddling across the floor and under the old green stove. Behind her, scurrying, was a tiny cricket. Or, no, it was another mouse— her child—a kidney bean come alive on the warped boards, and she too vanished under the stove. No cats here now to bring terror and death to them. No rancor in me that they might want my potato chips or white rice for the long eastern winter, to sustain them in what must be a kind of happiness, though surely not like our own arbitrary joys. Dark and small like those flecks of thought that blow like random ash along the edges of my head, so alien that I am always stunned—the complete faces, the odd sentences, not mine—not anything that I know or have known. With a better hand I could draw them in detail, but their logic I could never parse. In *The Secret Book of John* there are numbers that seem to have a great significance but are baffling. *The fifth is the kingdom of the fifth*, for instance, among all the numbers and their *archons* and secrets. And it's not Yahweh's fault in the long run either. *The Great Mother* gets saddled with the blame, as you might guess. Somehow her imperfect son is *her* fault. He was given mere fire and saw the angels under him and thought he was a Magnificent Being of Light. He creates an awful world. *But The Mother knew the abortion of darkness was imperfect.* Does this not terrify? I had to stop. In the end I settled on both the peaches *and* the gin. Then sitting at the table in the next room, the window so black it was a mirror, the table so scattered with papers and open books it was a reef of deeper confusions, that sound slipped in, the skittering, the scuttle, that tireless little beast returning, tooth and claw and hungry for something on the planks of the kitchen, the night growing long, like a stretched ribbon, like a road that a traveler stands on trying to remember what it was behind him that set him off with his armload of rude maps, and not even the cracked piece of a moon to read them by.

Black Notebook, Psalm 15, Dead Sea Scrolls, New Bedford

The fall sun on the pitched roof of the ancient schoolhouse across the street, its chimneys and skylights, gulls crying over on the docks, bricks and moldings all alight, and I was in the breeze and under the maple tree and the ivy wall watching Thomas and Peter and John raise the dead, sometimes in multitudes, and the pages shuffling now and then in the little gusts of wind up from the harbor. Every flower may be found here. Every temple withstands the dark cloud. Cobblestones ballasting the terrible ships from London, Liverpool, Lisbon, Barbados, Joppa, Tarshish. The old iron rails of the vanished trolleys, occulted in years of asphalt, uprising now, gleaming black as starlings as they slowly shoulder sunward again, and the starlings in the trees shivering the wind away and staring eternally into the one moment. Then down among the trawlers, all muscle and steel in their high freeboard, the palisades of scoured decks, the drags rolled, the hawsers lashed tight. *The Nancy Ann, The Sea Hag, Perpetua, Little Johnny, Eight Bells, Florabella, Sculley-Joe.* The Sunday Carillon proclaiming the rapture, searching for the resolving chord the way a certain kind of man might walk among that distant angelus feeling numbly for the one scrap of grammar that could make this world click suddenly into another world. Some junction that might be untouchable by death and indelible under the false joys of the empire. What makes all the old lies so beautiful? Simon Magus, it is told and told, was seen all over Rome, flying, by hundreds of upturned faces. But when he raised the dead it was a trick, and Peter made him fall and break his leg in three places, and he died later of the wounds in the care of a false healer. You cannot make this go away no matter how many wreathes you lay at the gray tombs. When I came home the back way, crossing and wandering the narrow streets, I passed a worn-down stone building that might have been a church once, hulking, the color of fog, and I walked into a group of men on the sidewalk. They seemed to be waiting for something. Some were smoking, some were sitting on the curb and on the steps of the building. Some were speaking Island Portuguese and Cape Verdean patois. I looked into their faces. Someone asked me how I was doing. All right, I said. All right. We talked until a red-faced man opened a big door from the inside, saying nothing, but the men slowly turned and shuffled up the steps. I stayed behind and thought about everything for a moment, but by then the light had lengthened in deep angles, golden from the west, and the wind had settled into a steady blow snapping some long flags on a nearby porch, and so I didn't go in.

Acknowledgments

The author wishes to thank the editors of the following magazines, in which versions of these poems first appeared.

AndarILAHgem (Azores, Portugal): "White Chair, Moonlight, Three A.M." (as "The White Chair")

Chautauqua: "When You Saw the Lightning"; "The Wild Swans"

Fourth River: "I Would Be True in My Own Body"; "Black Notebook, Day Six, Canadian Rockies"

Georgia Review: "These Are the Last Good Days of the Republic"; "I Wander Down My Street Because I Cannot Find a Book"

Kenyon Review: "The Sermon of Saint Anthony to the Fish"; "The Lesser Alleluia"; "September 10th—Black Notebook, Unnumbered"; "Black Notebook, Psalm 15, Dead Sea Scrolls, New Bedford"; "Are We Not Safe Here?"

Neo (Azores, Portugal): "Wail for Her"

Packing House Review: "The Marriage of Figaro"; "Sometimes God Saves the Fire"; "I Can See the Lapis Lazuli" (as "Dark Beautiful"); "Unable to Amend My Life I Begin Another Book"

Pearl: "I Piece Things Together"

PoetryMagazine.com: "June/July—11 Black Notebooks at the Desert Queen Motel"; "We Darken Things"

Prairie Schooner: "The Edge, Black Notebook #10, Desert Queen Motel" (as "The Edge")

Southern Review: "All Dharmas Are Marked With Emptiness"; "Sometimes I Can't Be Touched"

Tampa Review: "Sycamore"; "Saint Francis Blesses the Creatures"; "Late Rapturous"

Verdad: "Bicycle"

The author also wishes to thank the Hélio and Amélia Pedroso/Luso-American Foundation for the Endowed Chair in Portuguese and Portuguese-American Studies at the University of Massachusetts, Dartmouth. It was during this generous appointment that he wrote a number of these poems and put the book into its final form.

Notes

"The Sermon of Saint Anthony to the Fish": Title is from *The Sermon of Saint Anthony to the Fish and Other Texts*, António Vieira (1609-1697), translated from the Portuguese by Gregory Rabassa, Adamastor Books, Center for Portuguese Study and Culture, University of Massachusetts, Dartmouth, 2009.

Epigraph: From *The Relic*, José Maria de Eça de Queirós (1845-1900), translated from the Portuguese by Aubrey F.G. Bell, Max Reinhardt, London, 1954.

Description of the Lesser Alleluia is taken from *The New Roman Missal in Latin & English*, Benziger Brothers, U.S., 1937.

"Into the Second that Goes On Living": Title is taken from a line from Tomas Transtromer's poem, "Vermeer," translated by Steven Sondrup, in the journal *World Literature Today*, Volume 64, 1990.

"In Bed with an Old Book of Chinese Poetry": Title refers to *The Anchor Book of Chinese Poetry*, Tony Barnstone and Chou Ping, Knopf Doubleday, 2005.

"The Secret Book of John": Text is included in *The Other Bible*, Willis Barnstone, ed., Harper Collins, 1984.

"Psalm 15, Dead Sea Scrolls," refers to text included in *The Other Bible* (see above).

The Autumn House Poetry Series

MICHAEL SIMMS, GENERAL EDITOR

She Heads into the Wilderness Anne Marie Macari

When She Named Fire: An Anthology of Contemporary Poetry by American Women
    Andrea Hollander Budy, ed.

67 Mogul Miniatures Raza Ali Hasan

House Where a Woman Lori Wilson

A Theory of Everything Mary Crockett Hill • 2008, selected by Naomi Shihab Nye

What the Heart Can Bear Robert Gibb

The Working Poet: 75 Writing Exercises and a Poetry Anthology Scott Minar, ed.

Blood Honey Chana Bloch

The White Museum George Bilgere

The Gift That Arrives Broken Jacqueline Berger • 2009, selected by Alicia Ostriker

Farang Peter Blair

The Ghetto Exorcist James Tyner*

Where the Road Turns Patricia Jabbeh Wesley

Shake It and It Snows Gailmarie Pahmeier*

Crossing Laurel Run Maxwell King*

Coda Marilyn Donnelly

Shelter Gigi Marks*

The Autumn House Anthology of Contemporary American Poetry, 2nd ed.
    Michael Simms, ed.

To Make It Right Corrinne Clegg Hales • 2010, selected by Claudia Emerson

The Torah Garden Philip Terman

Lie Down With Me Julie Suk

The Beds Martha Rhodes

The Water Books Judith Vollmer

Sheet Music Robert Gibb

Natural Causes Brian Brodeur • 2011, selected by Denise Duhamel

Miraculum Ruth L. Schwartz

Late Rapturous Frank X. Gaspar

• Winner of the annual Autumn House Poetry Prize

* *Coal Hill Review* chapbook series

Design and Production

Cover and text design by Chiquita Babb

Cover photo: iStockphoto

Author photo: Dave Terrell

Text set in Fournier, a font designed by Pierre Simon Fournier circa 1742, then revived in 1924 by Stanley Morison for the Monotype Corporation

Printed by McNaughton & Gunn on 55# Glatfelter Natural Offset Antique